FARM TRACTORS
IN COLOUR

FARM TRACTORS

IN COLOUR

Text © 1996 Liz Purser
Design and layout © 1996 Promotional Reprint Company Ltd.
Published 1996 by the Promotional Reprint Company Ltd, Kiln House, 210 New Kings Road, London SW6 4NZ.

ISBN 1 85648 395 9

Printed and bound in China.

PREFACE

Ever since man moved from hunter-gatherer to farmer he has searched for ways to improve the speed at which basic manual jobs could be performed more quickly and efficiently: ploughing sowing, tilling, seeding, harvesting, threshing, baling – all the backbreaking essentials. The invention of the steam engine provided the first major breakthrough: steam-driven agricultural implements made for major and immediate improvement to the farmer's lot at the end of the 18th century, but it was with the internal combustion engine that the farmer received a dependable, easily maintained and manufactured power unit. The first tractor was probably the Charter made at Sterling Illinois in 1889 by the Charter Gas Engine Co; it powered a threshing machine.

Tractors changed rapidly from power units to prime movers once suitable engines – petrol at first then diesel – became available. World War 1 saw a massive need for something to make up for the loss of manpower to the trenches and by the time the landsmen were out of khaki a revolution had taken place.

Cheaper production methods meant that tractors became available to the small farmer and not just the big rich ones and by the time another world war came along, the tractor was an essential item of farm equipment. Today few farmers could get by without one of these maids-of-all-work and the competition to provide them with not only the best tractor, but every conceivable labour-saving add-on, has meant that the construction of farm tractors and agricultural machinery is a major business. Technically, tractors needed to be able to run as well as pull agricultural implements, something made easier when International Harvester developed a power take-off mechanism so that equipment could be driven while the tractor was moving, thus allowing implements to be

powered at a constant speed by the tractor's engine. These early tractors' iron wheels were all of the same size, but it soon became usual for the front wheels to be smaller than those at the rear. The wheels were always broad, in order to carry the tractor's weight without sinking, in conditions where the ground was soft. The front wheels were often ridged or grooved around the circumference to assist steering, while the rear wheels usually featured crosswise slats, called 'spuds' or 'lugs', which provided grip.

The problem of poor grip on soft ground was solved by means of an endless belt fitted with slats, which passed around both the front and rear wheels, which is now commonly known as a 'crawler'; the trade name of 'caterpillar' is often given to this type of tractor. Road regulations made it difficult to take iron-wheeled or crawler tractors onto public roads, however. The American Firestone Tire and Rubber Company's development of pneumatic rubber tyres (which were first used in 1932 by Allis-Chalmers tractors) was therefore very significant. From then on, it was common for tractors to be fitted with large tyres with rubber lugs, thus providing a good grip on both road and land.

By 1935, Irishman Harry Ferguson's earlier innovation of three-point linkage equipment (which allowed implements to be attached to tractors), was supplemented by a complementary hydraulic system which was suitable for a wide variety of farm implements. This was worked by means of levers situated near the driver's seat, and enabled implements and heavy loads to be lifted or lowered easily. A verbal agreement between Ford and Ferguson in 1938 later led to a bitter legal dispute between the two companies and, by 1945, Ferguson had returned to England to make tractors in Coventry with the Standard Motor Co.

In 1941, the American president, F. D. Roosevelt, pushed through the Lend-Lease Act under which, for the duration of World War 2, the US supplied Britain with warships and other equipment vital to the war effort, including agricultural machinery. Thousands of extra tractors were accordingly received, and combine harvesters made their first appearance in British fields.

The larger, more powerful, postwar tractors significantly reduced the time needed for many farm activities. They were, however, expensive, and were designed for large farms. As a result, many small farms which were unable to afford these machines found themselves unable to compete; many were subsequently bought up, family farms declined, and the number of workers also fell. Nevertheless, the 1947 Agricultural Act, along with various grants available to farmers, served to increase their confidence, and gave them a sense of security.

The 1950s was a period during which the economy was rebuilt, food was in short supply, and towns expanded into the countryside. Pressure was put on farmers to produce more and cheaper food on a smaller amount of land. They began to invest in new machinery, and science and technology began to prevail in farming.

Today's modern, multipurpose tractors are large and complex machines that show no signs of reaching the end of their development. Four-wheel drive has been vastly improved during the past decade or so, and hydraulically operated implements that can be attached, towed, or fitted are common. The majority of leading tractor manufacturers across the US, the UK and Europe fit their machines with clutchless gear changes, or use synchromesh gearboxes that are operated by means of a short, hydraulic control lever, along with a similar lever that enables forward-to-reverse changes for loader work. Most are also fitted with fully electronic instruments, their built-in microprocessors allowing optional automatic operation of electrohydraulic controls (this is more efficient and safer than manual operation).

Now that tractors can deliver preset applications of fertiliser, planting and sowing have become mechanically precise operations; similarly, harvesting has seen great changes. The risk of the loss or failure of a crop is now comparatively slight and, thanks to modern-day tractors, all processes take place at a much faster rate, and with a great reduction in the amount of labour required.

Driver comfort and safety have also received much attention: several government regulations have aimed to reduce serious tractor accidents and to protect the health and welfare of their drivers, while rollbars have long been a means of minimising injuries in accidents caused by tractors turning over. Today's tractor operators sit in air-conditioned safety cabs, whose sound insulation protects their hearing and reduces fatigue. High-class, suspended seats that lessen the tractor's vibration, adjustable steering columns that allow the operator to alter both their length and angle, not to mention today's well-positioned controls, have all made a valuable contribution to the driver's ability to work long hours at peak periods, without suffering any corresponding loss of alertness. Furthermore, some tractors can easily transfer automatic records of work rates, areas covered, fuel used, and so on, to the farm-office's management computer.

Computer technology has not only helped to create highly technical and sophisticated tractors and other types of farm machinery, but has also instigated a dramatic change in their design methods. Although tractors have attained their present important position in world agriculture because of their low working costs, their efficient cultivation ability, their reliability and their production of more and better crops, research and development continues apace, thus doubtless heralding further developments in tractor manufacture in order to meet the changing needs of future markets.

ABOVE: This Bamfords disc harrow is starting to prepare a seedbed for another crop. The angle of each gang of discs can be altered; increasing the angle creates a finer tilth but requires more traction. It was one of the earliest machines to be hydraulically folded for road transport and storage.

RIGHT: Reciprocating-knife grass-cutters usually employed a single reciprocating knife bar fitted with many blades, which cut the crop against a stationary blade. However, this example, Busatis' BM 324 KW, had two sets of knives, working not unlike a pair of scissors.

BUSATIS

THE MODERN THREE-POINT LINKAGE
MOWER WITH DOUBLE-KNIFE CUTTER BAR

DOPPEL MESSER **BM 324 KW**

BUSATIS DOUBLE-KNIFE MOWERS UNRIVALLED FOR CAPACITY

ABOVE: A Case 2090 tractor, marketed by David Brown/Case in the early 1980s. This two-wheel drive (2wd) vehicle developed 120hp (89kW) and was one of the largest of its time. This size of tractor is common today, although most would now be 4wd.

RIGHT: Today this cab looks cluttered, but at the time it was built it featured many significant advances, including a flat floor area and comfortable, adjustable seats.

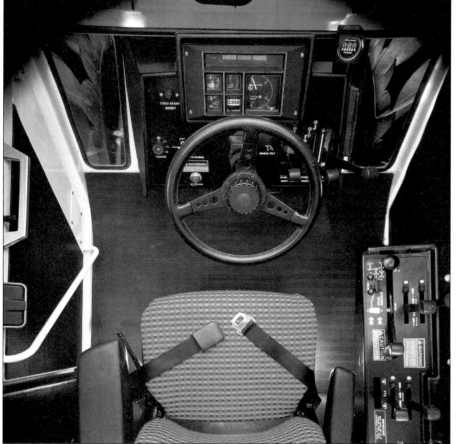

ABOVE: The Case 4690 tractor, again marketed in the early 1980s, had a six-cylinder turbo-charged diesel engine which developed 233hp (174kW). The transmission gave three forward gears that could be changed on the move by means of a semi-automatic powershift gearbox in each of four speed ranges, giving 12 forward gears altogether. The steering options were: turning the front or rear wheels only; co-ordinated steering, where the front and rear wheels point in different directions; and crab steering, where all wheels point in the same direction and the tractor turns sideways.

ABOVE: The CLAAS MEGA combine harvester range, available with cutterbar widths of 4.5m to 6.6m. They are fitted with either Mercedes-Benz or Perkins engines of between 118kW (160hp) and 199kW (270hp). The hydrostatic-drive system is used on all models giving infinitely variable forward speeds.

BELOW: To maximise the machine's usable time, movement between fields and along roads must be as easy and as fast as possible. This picture shows the table folded for road transport, allowing easy movement through farm gateways.

RIGHT: The cab of the MEGA range combine harvester has the maximum possible surface area of glass, so giving good visibility on both sides as well as to the front. This is essential for wide cutter-bars.

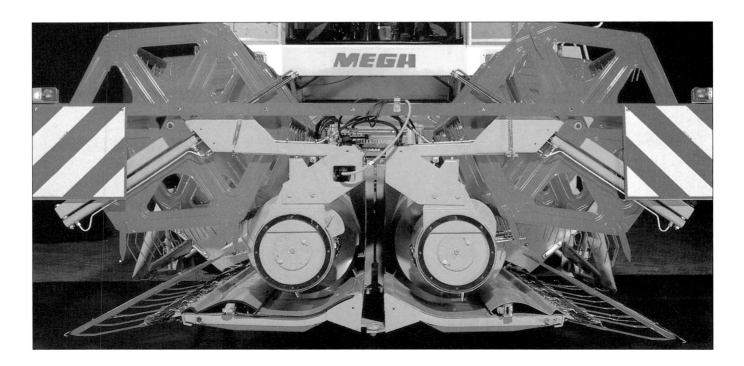

LEFT: The interior of the MEGA combine harvester's cab has all its major controls on the right-hand side of the driver — forward and reverse; speed; cutterbar and reel positions; and automatic controls for presetting the cutterbar height and the table-contour following device. The console also gives information on machine settings, travel speeds and provides throughout monitoring.

RIGHT: Most combine harvesters are used in wheat, barley or oat fields, but harvesting maize requires a different header. Other adaptations will harvest grass seed, sunflowers, oil seed, rape, peas, beans and linseed.

LEFT: Combine harvesters do not work efficiently on sloping ground. This machine can be equipped with an automatic compensation system fitted to the upper sieve box in order to minimise the problems associated with such conditions.

ABOVE: A high-capacity auger empties the full grain tank into a trailer alongside. The trailer is towed beside the combine while harvesting continues.

15

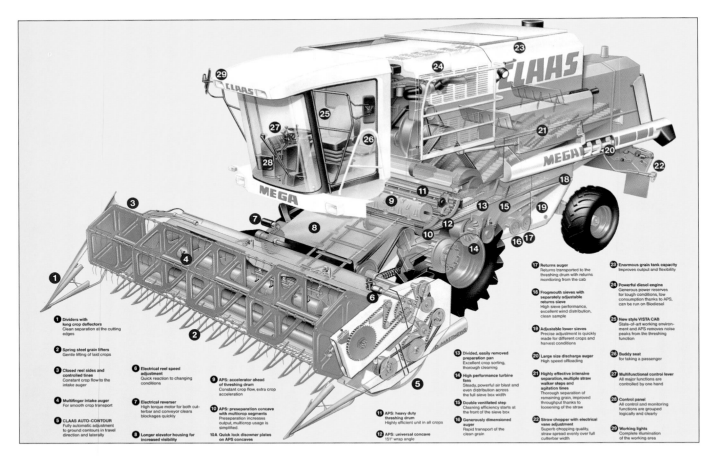

1 Dividers with long crop deflectors
Clean separation at the cutting edges

2 Spring steel grain lifters
Gentle lifting of laid crops

3 Closed reel sides and controlled tines
Constant crop flow to the intake auger

4 Multifinger intake auger
For smooth crop transport

5 CLAAS AUTO-CONTOUR
Fully automatic adjustment to ground contours in travel direction and laterally

6 Electrical reel speed adjustment
Quick reaction to changing conditions

7 Electrical reverser
High torque motor for both cutterbar and conveyor clears blockages quickly

8 Longer elevator housing for increased visibility

9 APS: accelerator ahead of threshing drum
Constant crop flow, extra crop acceleration

10 APS: preseparation concave with multicrop segments
Preseparation increases output, multicrop usage is simplified.

10A Quick lock disowner plates on APS concaves

11 APS: heavy duty threshing drum
Highly efficient unit in all crops

12 APS: universal concave
151° wrap angle

13 Divided, easily removed preparation pan
Excellent crop sorting, thorough cleaning

14 High performance turbine fans
Steady, powerful air blast and even distribution across the full sieve box width

15 Double ventilated step
Cleaning efficiency starts at the front of the sieve box

16 Generously dimensioned auger
Rapid transport of the clean grain

17 Returns auger
Returns transported to the threshing drum with returns monitoring from the cab

18 Frogmouth sieves with separately adjustable returns sieve
High sieve performance, excellent wind distribution, clean sample

19 Adjustable lower sieves
Precise adjustment is quickly made for different crops and harvest conditions

20 Large size discharge auger
High speed offloading

21 Highly effective intensive separation, multiple straw walker steps and agitation tines
Thorough separation of remaining grain, improved throughput thanks to loosening of the straw

22 Straw chopper with electrical vane adjustment
Superb chopping quality, straw spread evenly over full cutterbar width

23 Enormous grain tank capacity
Improves output and flexibility

24 Powerful diesel engine
Generous power reserves for tough conditions, low consumption thanks to APS, can be run on Biodiesel

25 New style VISTA CAB
State-of-art working environment and APS removes noise peaks from the threshing function

26 Buddy seat
for taking a passenger

27 Multifunctional control lever
All major functions are controlled by one hand

28 Control panel
All control and monitoring functions are grouped logically and clearly

29 Working lights
Complete illumination of the working area

ABOVE: This diagram shows the internal workings and features of the CLAAS MEGA range of combine harvesters when fitted with a conventional header.

BELOW: The CLAAS JAGUAR self-propelled precision-chop harvester is designed to pick up the grass, cut it very short and blow it into a trailer being towed alongside. This is important when silage-making, because short grass compacts well, so making better quality and more easily handled silage.

ABOVE: Another view of the CLAAS JAGUAR harvester.

BELOW: A CLAAS JAGUAR 880 self-propelled precision chop, fitted with an eight-row maize header. Each maize plant is cut by a pair of cutting discs, and is then held and fed into the feed auger by a pair of feed chains. The machine automatically steers itself, using a pair of sensors situated in front of the cutting discs.

ABOVE: The ergonomically designed cab of the Deutz-Fahr AgroStar tractor is mounted on shock-absorbing rubber blocks to reduce vibration. Unusually, most of the controls are on the driver's right, so making access to the cab easier.

RIGHT and FAR RIGHT: The Deutz-Fahr AgroStar tractor, a 4wd machine, is seen pulling a Lemken reversible plough. This tractor is also fitted with front-mounted linkage so that it can operate two implements in one pass: for example a cultivator on the front and a seed drill at the rear.

ABOVE: The world's first self-propelled big square baler, the Deutz-Fahr PowerPress is ideal for the contractor who bales and moves large quantities of straw, hay and silage. Its hydrostatic drive gives infinitely variable forward speed. Pick-up is available in three working widths: 3m, 6.4m, and 8.4m. Bales of 1.2m width by 0.85m height are produced with adjustable lengths, usually c2m.

BELOW: The PowerPress can be supplied with a bale trailer, which collects and stacks bales as they are ejected. Closed-circuit TV is also an option, so that the driver knows that all is well at the back as well as the front. Clearing up to 100 bales an hour, the wider version is ideally suited to large areas of flat ground.

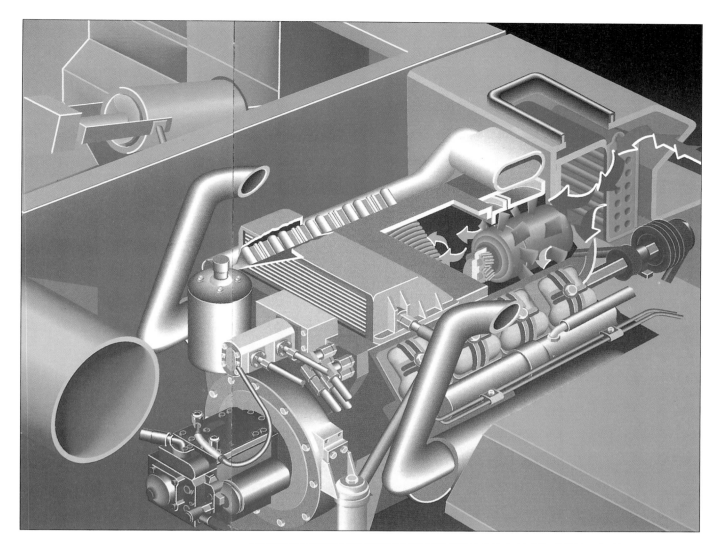

ABOVE: A 228kW (310hp) V8 diesel engine is powering hydraulic pumps for the main power functions of this Deutz-Fahr TopLiner. Also shown is the grain tank, with a capacity of 8,500cu m. The harvested grain is held here prior to discharge.

RIGHT: The Topliner's cab is ergonomically designed, with all its controls carefully positioned to ensure driver comfort and to minimise fatigue. The air-conditioned, dust-free cab is also sound insulated and has excellent visibility through tinted glass.

ABOVE: Deutz-Fahr's 4075 HTS is working well in a standing crop. It can be fitted with different front ends (tables) to give an effective cutting width of 5.4.m to 6.6.m. These can be quickly and easily removed and, for road transport, are towed on a trailer behind the combine. Even so, the machine is still 3.5m wide.

RIGHT: The StarLiner cab has an electronic monitoring system for the engine and machine functions and shaft speeds. This will alert the driver should a malfunction occur during operation.

FAR RIGHT: Smaller and less powerful than the TopLiners, these machines are available with different tables to give cutting widths of 3-5.4m. The complete machine weighs about 8 tonnes and is fitted with a 110 or 118kW (150 or 160hp) engine.

The Deutz-Fahr 120 was fitted
with an air-cooled, six-cylinder
Deutz diesel engine developing
81kW (110hp). The transmission
gave 20 forward and five reverse
gears, with synchronisation
available for on-the-move gear
changing.

ABOVE: The PowerLiner is the baby of the Deutz-Fahr range, with engines from 85-95kW (116-135hp). It has the technology of the TopLiner, but suits the farmer who prefers to bring in his own harvest instead of depending on contracting companies.

RIGHT: To relieve the PowerLiner's driver from having to carry out constant checks, the 22 most important functions, from engine temperature to drum speed, are monitored. The failsafe principle of Deutz-Fahr Agrotronic ensures continuous and accurate information.

ABOVE: The Fiat 1880 DT, marketed during the early 1980s in this country, had 4wd and a 134kW (180hp) six-cylinder direct injection turbo-charged diesel engine. Transmission consisted of a dry single-plate clutch, and 12 forward and four reverse speeds, all synchronised. Power take off (PTO) was driven through a wet multiplate hydraulically operated clutch to give a 540 or 1,000rpm shaft speed. Brakes were also of the wet multidisc type and were hydraulically operated.

ABOVE RIGHT: The Fendt 104S 4wd 41kW (55hp) three-cylinder, direct-injection diesel tractor. For normal driving it was fitted with a dry single-plate clutch, which drove Fendt's 'turbomatic' clutch. (Sometimes called fluid fly wheels.) These have the advantage of absorbing shock loads in the transmission system — here including the PTO — drive and providing a smooth take-up of drive. The gearbox had 13 forward and four reverse gears.

RIGHT: Produced in the mid-1970s, the cab of the Fendt 104S is shown here. It is interesting to compare this with the modern equivalent. Today's operator has more space, a better seat (though this one was good at the time) and controls that are neatly and ergonomically laid out.

ABOVE: An early 1980s Model 6610 Ford tractor, powered by a Ford four-cylinder diesel engine which developed 64kW (86hp). The gearbox was of a column-change design, giving eight forward and four reverse gears. This was not successful, as the driver did not know which gear he was in by looking at the gear levers. A 'dual power' option was available for the gearbox, which doubled the number of speeds. This was an electrically operated hydraulic clutch pack, which controlled a planetary reduction unit.

RIGHT: Ford Series 70.

RIGHT: The Ford series 20 compact range consists of five tractors of 12-30kW (16.7-41.3hp). Shown here are the 1720 33hp and the 2120 45hp models. Different transmissions, including hydrostatic on the two smaller models, give an infinite range of forward and reverse speeds. This series of tractors is suitable for light work, and they are often fitted with grassland tyres (tyres without ribs) so that they can work without damaging the surface of the grass. These low-powered tractors need to be fitted with a rollbar to protect the driver if the tractor overturns. The left-hand tractor (1720) has a planter mounted on the rear linkage, while the right (2120) is operating a horizontal rotor cultivator to prepare the seedbed.

BELOW: The four tractors in the Ford series 70 range from 125kW to 179kW (170-240hp). The clutchless, electronically controlled gear changes will give 18 forward and nine reverse speeds; these can be doubled with the optional creeper box. For road transport, once tenth gear has been reached, a button can be pressed and the transmission becomes completely automatic, changing up and down according to the load on the engine.

ABOVE: The Ford 8770, pulling a nine-furrow semi-mounted reversible plough. The hydraulic system has a lift capacity of nearly 8.9 tonnes on the link-arm end; such lift capacity is essential for large implements. An electronically operated draft-control system controls the operating depth and rate of drop. Once the controls have been set, the maximum height and depth are also fixed

RIGHT: The business end of an 8870 — the 210hp 7.5litre six-cylinder turbocharged diesel engine featuring air-to-air intercooling.

TOP: Ford Model 2120 compact with a 41.3hp water-cooled diesel engine — a growing market.

ABOVE: From the International 88 series, this model 3588 is fitted with a 132kW (177hp) six-cylinder engine. An early 1980s tractor, it was articulated (pivoted in the middle) to achieve steering.

ABOVE: The International 785 XL tractor, available in two-or four-wheel drive versions (2wd is shown here), is shown powering a Rotorvator, producing a seedbed for a following crop. It featured a redesigned cab to improve the working environment for the driver. This was a significant improvement on earlier models.

RIGHT: The JCB 526-55 Loadall Telescopic Handler. These machines are ideal for many on-farm handling duties. There are both rear-wheel steered or four-wheel steer, versions, with four-wheel drive and four equal-sized large-diameter wheels. The boom is telescopic, which enables the machine to pick up or place loads some distance in front of it. It will lift 2.6 tonnes to a height of 5.5m with a retracted boom, and 1 tonne when the boom is extended to 3.05m. A wide variety of front-end attachments is available.

ABOVE: The JCB 4145 Farm Master. This centre-pivot articulated loader is suitable for many loading jobs on the farm — silage-making, muck-handling etc. It has four-wheel drive with automatic powershift transmission, driven from the engine in a torque converter. Oil-immersed hydraulically operated brakes work on all four wheels.

RIGHT: JCB's 409 Telemaster loader is a pivot-steer telescopic handler which will lift 2 tonnes to 4.3m, and will deliver a 1 tonne load to a maximum reach of 2.86m in front of the machine. An extensive range of front-end attachments is available, including the manure grab shown, pallet forks, conventional and side-tip shovels, crane jib and

sweepers. The 71kW (96hp) engine drives a fully synchromesh gearbox with integral torque converter and electrically operated powershift reversing shuttle for smooth forward/reverse gear changes. A safe-load indicator in the cab gives a progressive readout of the machine's forward stability.

These revolutionary JCB Fastrac tractors, launched in 1991, are fitted with 'soft' suspension and self-levelling systems. The smallest in the range has an engine rated at 86kW (115hp), while the largest is 127kW (170hp). The transmission provides 36 forward and 12 reverse gears, and a hydraulic lift capacity of 7,000kg is at the link end of the largest model. Apart from normal agricultural work, they are designed for high-speed road work. The 115hp Fastrac 1115 can haul a 24-tonne gross train weight (a 14-tonne payload) at 50kph.

ABOVE: The Fastrac 185 pulling a reversible plough.

BELOW: The tractor spraying.

ABOVE: The JCB Robot 165 skid steer loader is unusual in that it obtains its steering by disconnecting the hydrostatic drive to the wheels on one side of the machine, while continuing to power the other side. The machine then skids round the corner, hence its name. Highly manoeuvrable for its size, it will lift a heavy load — 650kg.

RIGHT: The 926 is the smaller of two rough-terrain fork lifts produced by JCB, having a nominal lift capacity of 2.6 tonnes. It can be fitted with different masts to give working heights of 3.6-6.55m. The machine here is shown fitted with a bale grab, handling small rectangular bales. It has 4wd rear-wheel steer and is fitted with an electrically operated reversing shuttle for smooth gear changes.

ABOVE: The 412S Farm Master Servoplus wheeled loading shovel is fitted with a turbocharged 82kW (110hp) Perkins diesel engine, which powers an automatic full-powershift transmission through a single-stage torque converter. A full range of front-end attachments is available, covering the job requirements of agriculture, warehousing and forestry. The machine illustrated is fitted with a grain bucket.

RIGHT: JCB's 2C XL 4x4x4 Farm Master has four equal-sized wheels, four-wheel drive and four-wheel steering. The fact that the front and rear axles both steer reduces the turning circle and

makes the machine very manoeuvrable. Maximum lift capacity, when fitted with a general purpose shovel, is

4,860kg. The illustration shows a machine fitted with a manure grab, cleaning out an old stock building.

ABOVE: Hillmaster slope levelling system in operation.

RIGHT: Five John Deere Z series combine harvesters, fitted with straw choppers/spreaders at the rear, working together. A field has to be particularly large to justify a line-up like this.

BELOW: A John Deere Z Series 2066, standing stationary whilst unloading. The unloading rate is 70 litres/sec, and is usually carried out on the move. The cutting width may be 4.25-7.60m, depending on the table selected. The machine is fitted with a 199kW (270hp) John Deere engine.

ABOVE: The Z series combine harvesters can be fitted with a 'Hillmaster Slope Levelling System'. This raises or lowers one wheel and the front plate of the straw elevator (to the rear of the table), thus keeping the whole of the combine vertical on slopes up to 11%, while the cutter bar follows ground level.

BELOW: A cutaway view of the Z series John Deere combine (not including the table) showing: 1. straw elevator, 2. threshing drum, 2a. rear beater, 3. concave, 4. grain pan, 5. sieves, 6. fan, 7. straw walkers, 8. engine, 9. unloading auger, which swings outwards.

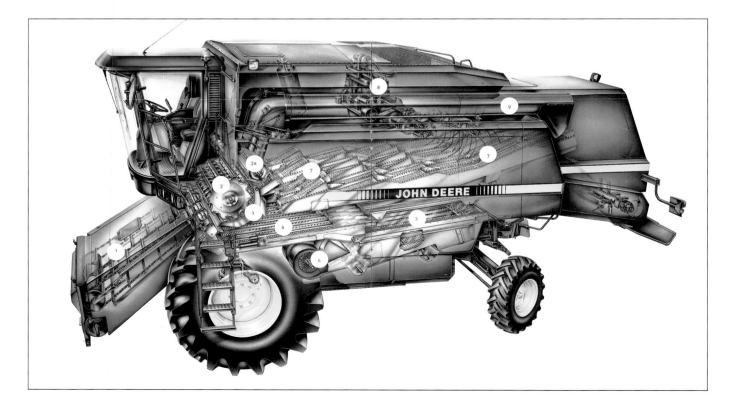

RIGHT: John Deere makes its own engines. This six-cylinder version, as fitted to combine harvesters, is shown driving a hydraulic pump. The oil from this pump is used to drive hydraulic motors to propel the machine, giving an infinite range of forward speeds. The harvesting and threshing mechanism is belt driven.

New 136-kW (185-hp) 8100

New 155-kW (210-hp) 8200

New 170-kW (230-hp) 8300

New 191-kW (260-hp) 8400

ABOVE: A line-up of the John Deere 8000 series tractors from 136kW (185hp) to 191kW (260hp). Because of their size, these tractors are suitable solely for the larger arable farm or contractor. All have four-wheel drive.

RIGHT: The excellent view from the 8000 series tractors comes courtesy of a single piece front windscreen without centreline or beltline seams.

ABOVE: The 8000 series steering column both tilts and is telescopic, to make driver access easier. After moving, it always returns to its previous setting.

RIGHT: The panel for secondary monitoring and instrumentation. The left-hand screen can display percentage wheelslip and compare true and actual ground speed with the optional radar system. It will also give power take-off, speed, engine hours run and other information. The right-hand screen allows hydraulic rate and flow to be electronically set.

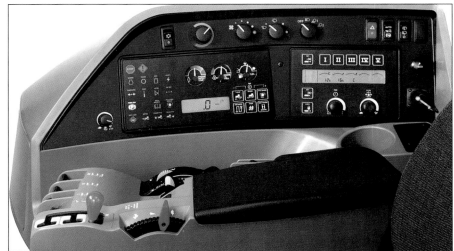

This can be continuous, timed or on the operation of a lever. Other controls mainly relate to those found on most cars.

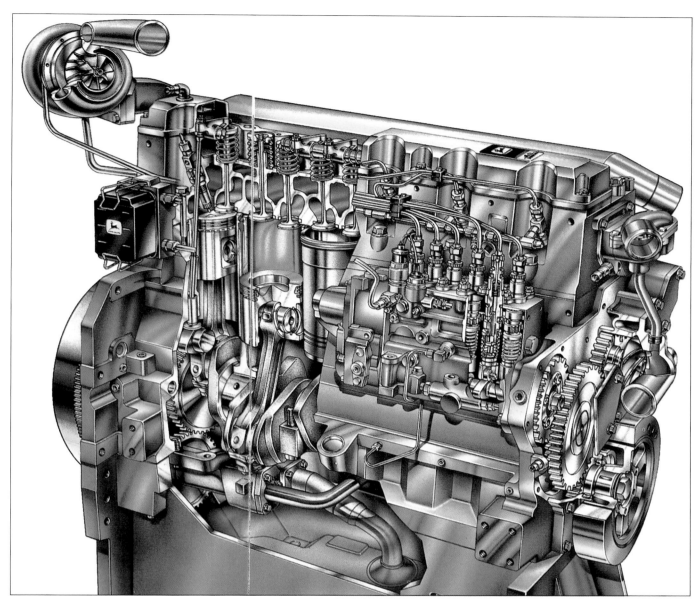

ABOVE: An engine from one of the John Deere 8000 tractor series. These six cylinder direct-injection turbocharged engines are electronically controlled.

RIGHT: The 8000 series features a 'Field Cruise' engine-control system, which automatically maintains engine speed by means of programmed fuel delivery.

Cutaway view of the John Deere 8400 tractor

1 Cooling fan and radiator
2 Engine
3 Gearbox with 16 forward and
  5 reverse speeds
4 Final drive and differential

5 Planetary speed-reduction unit
6 Front axle drive and differential
7 Flexible drive-shaft joint
8 Hub-mounted planetary speed
  reduction unit

9 The 'TechCentre' cab, offering
  significantly more than room
  than previous models. It is
  heated and air-conditioned

ABOVE and BELOW LEFT: 8000 series tractors.

BELOW: The John Deere 6400 tractor engine produces 76kW (104hp). It can be supplied with two different versions of power-shift transmission, both of which are available with a creeper option. It is also available with a conventional synchromesh transmission in three versions, again with a creeper option.

ABOVE: The four- wheel drive 7800 tractor from the John Deere range is pulling a cultivator after the corn has been harvested. This 125kW (170hp) six cylinder diesel-engine tractor is fitted with an oil-cooled, maintenance-free clutch, and either a powershift or a synchromesh system.

RIGHT: The John Deere 4wd 3400 tractor, is the largest in the 3000 series. The engine develops 63kW (85hp) and is fitted with a four-cylinder turbo-charged diesel engine (unlike the others). The cab heights are under 2.5m so that they can be used inside buildings. The bonnets and cabs are designed to give the good visibility from the driver's seat.

ABOVE: John Deere high-density large square baler, model 690, will produce a bale of 120x80cms and between 1 and 2.5m long. These large square bales are ideal for maximising transport payloads, which is important where long road-haulage distances are involved.

RIGHT: The JD 4240S, a 140hp (104kW) six-cylinder turbocharged tractor, fitted with a hydraulically operated wet (oil-immersed) transmission clutch and a gearbox that gives 16 forward and six reverse speeds.

ABOVE: The JD 4240S tractor, dating from the early 1980s, is seen here with a light, rigid-tine cultivator and serrated discs, the implement being momentarily out of operation and supported on the tractor's hydraulic three-point linkage. This range of tractors used an unusual 'closed centre' hydraulic system, which necessitated the fitting of different control valves on ancillary hydraulic equipment operated by the machine.

RIGHT: John Deere Model 3400.

ABOVE: John Deere Model 6400.

LEFT: The KUHN Gyrotedder spreads and fluffs up previously cut grass to promote rapid drying as part of the haymaking process. This machine has an 8.5m working width, and can be hydraulically folded for road transport. It can cover up to one ha (2.5 acres) in less than 10 minutes.

KUHN's Gyrorake GA 4501, a
single-rotor rake, has 13 tine arms
which rake the dried grass into a
single swath so that it can be
picked up by a baler. The tines
automatically retract once the
grass is in the swath so that it
cannot be dragged back out again.

ABOVE: This four-furrow plough from KUHN's Master series is reversible, so that when the driver reaches the end of the field, he can turn it over and use the other four bodies to come back up the field alongside the work just completed. The bodies may have an effective working width of 14" or 16" (350-400mm).

RIGHT: The KUHN Venta pneumatic cultivator/seeder, HR 4002, consists of a vertical tined power harrow which works in front of a crumbler roller. Seed is blown into grooves that are made behind this. An unusual feature of this machine is the hopper; it slides down to the rear for easy filling.

RIGHT: Lamborghini Premium Model 1050.

BELOW: A maximum of 77kW (104hp) is produced by the six-cylinder diesel engine of the Lamborghini Premium 1060. The gearbox has four forward-range speeds: creeper, low, medium and high, each with five gears giving 20 individual speed bands from 200m-40kph. The 4wd tractor illustrated has front-end weights to balance it when heavy rear implements are fitted. An onboard computer monitors draft and wheelslip when ploughing.

LEFT: Brochure for an early Leyland Nuffield 154.— 1960s luxury!

CENTRE LEFT: Agricultural tractors have long been adapted and used for non-agricultural purposes. This machine is from the Leyland 700/800 series. Fitted at the rear with highway tyres, this reduces the amount of wear that takes place when working on a hard surface. Some manufacturers supplied tractors as skid units (no wheels, front axle or cab) to power other purpose-built machines.

BOTTOM LEFT: The Leyland 702 (2wd) and 704 (4wd) agricultural tractors. Both models were fitted with a four-cylinder direct-injection naturally aspirated diesel engine. The hydraulic system was 'live', i.e. hydraulic power was available at all times from an engine-driven pump. A disadvantage with older tractors of many different makes was that when the clutch pedal was depressed, the drive to the hydraulic pump, as well as the transmission was disengaged.

TOP and ABOVE: There are 13 models of these rubber-tracked crawler tractors, manufactured by Morooka of Japan, with engines ranging from 30kW to 250kW (41hp to 337hp). They are designed to work in very soft ground conditions, as above showing cultivation work in operation in a rice paddy field. Some operations may be carried out in poor ground conditions, or where soil compaction must be avoided.

ABOVE: This rubber-tracked Morooka crawler tractor is harvesting maize for silage, or for direct feeding to cattle. This is done in the autumn, when the ground is often wet.

LEFT: Morooka rotary plow in action.

ABOVE: Maschio/Sulky 'up and over' drill combining harrow and drill together.

BELOW: Made in Italy, the Maschio Recotiller consists of a number of gear-driven rotors, each fitted with two vertically mounted blades. The rotors rotate to break down soil clods after initial cultivation. A crumbler roller, also attached to the machine, completes the process. The Recotiller illustrated here consists of two 3m sections, each with 12 rotors, which fold for road transport. A wide range of narrower machines are also available. The tractor is a Ford 8770.

ABOVE: Massey Ferguson 362.

LEFT: This Massey Ferguson tractor is fitted with a heavy-duty loader as standard. The transmission is capable of repeated forward/reverse changes, with the minimum of wear and operator fatigue. The transmission has a powershift between forward and reverse, and four forward and four reverse speeds; synchromesh allows on-the-move gear-changing. 4 wheel drive can be electronically engaged. A variety of attachments are available for the front loader, and a fork lift is illustrated. Various grabs, buckets and a big bale spike can also be fitted.

LEFT: The MF 8100 series consists of six tractors ranging from 145 to 211hp (108kW to 155kW). A cutaway view of the MF 8160 4wd tractor, the largest tractor in the series, is shown.

(1) The engine drives the gearbox through an oil-cooled multiple clutch.

(2) The gearbox is MF's Dynashift unit, which gives four powershift changes in each of the eight synchronised gears, making a total of 32 forward and 32 reverse gears.

(3) The gearbox drives a crown wheel, which has a differential unit attached to it. The differential allows one wheel to go faster than the other for cornering. Each drive shaft to the wheels has its speed decreased and torque increased by an epicyclic reduction unit

(4) Drive to the front axle is through a similar crown wheel, and differential (5), as well as a hub reduction unit (6).

LEFT: This 170hp (125kW) MF 8140 tractor is fitted with the same clutch and transmission system as the 8160. It is shown operating a powered cultivator/drill combination. It is fitted with dual wheels at the rear, to minimise soil compaction.

RIGHT: A MF series 8100 cab which has access from either side of the tractor. As is now common practice, most of the controls are on the driver's right, and the cab is spacious, with an uncluttered and flat floor area.

BELOW: MF 8110 and 6120 tractors working in tandem.

ABOVE: The MF Auto Level combine harvester automatically keeps the entire body level when working across sloping fields of up to 11 degrees. This keeps an even spread of material across the full width of all the machine's grain-separating components, and reduces grain losses. Levelling is automatically achieved by pivoting the transmission final-drive units about the transmission shafts from the gearbox. The table automatically maintains an even cutting height across its full width, controlled by mechanical ground sensors.

INSET: Shows how levelling is achieved. Note the relative positions of the final-drive units.

RIGHT: The MF 40 combine harvester working in a clean crop of standing corn, with the straw chopper in operation.

RIGHT: Shown here is the cab of the 30/40 series combine. All the functions are electrically or electronically controlled. There are no handles, rod and linkage controls or hydraulic spool blocks in the cab, making it very different from earlier machines. The 'Datavision' screen provides the driver with information on the combine's performance, settings and service requirements. It can also be linked to a satellite GPS (global positioning system), so that yield maps can be created of individual fields. Fertiliser and, if necessary, trace-element applications, can then be delivered on the areas of the field needing attention.

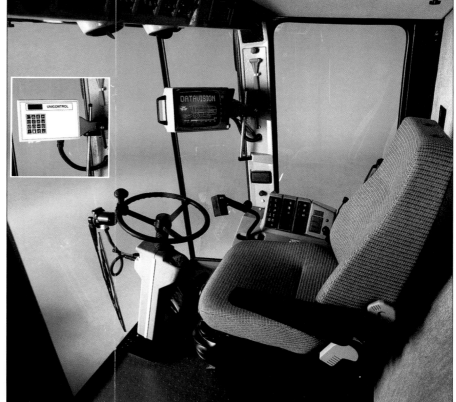

ABOVE: MF 900 series parallel-lift loader. These include attachments designed to fit most of the current MF range of tractors. The largest of the loader range can exert a tear-out force of 3700kg, and will lift 1400kg to a full working height. The range includes digging buckets, manure forks, silage grabs, palette forks, bag hooks and bale grabs.

RIGHT: A wide range of tractors have been adapted for work in orchards and other unusual situations. The MF 304 series S & F model 394F is illustrated. All have a reduced track width compared to normal machines. Some feature an extended wheelbase to improve longitudinal stability, making them suitable for hillside and alpine conditions. Others are low profile, with a folding rollbar, for working under low branches.

ABOVE: A wide variety of specialist machinery is available to fit behind the narrow MF 304 series, including crop dusters, and, shown here, a rotary mower for keeping weeds down. This one is unusual, in that the right cutter head will cut in between the plants, and when the curved feeler bar touches the next plant, the cutter head swings back and only returns when the plant has been passed.

RIGHT: An MF 362 tractor fitted with an 810 loader. The feeding and bedding of housed animals was transformed by the introduction of the large round bale, and the means to move them mechanically. Movements of hay and straw used to be carried out by hand when the small rectangular bales were all that was available.

BELOW: This MF 3120 tractor has been fitted with a seed and fertiliser hopper on the front, and a power harrow/drill unit to the rear. This arrangement distributes the total weight more equally over all the wheels. Dual wheels, front and rear, minimise compaction.

TOP RIGHT: Marketed in the mid 1970s, before the days of factory fitted cabs, drivers of MF 515 combines were subjected to noise from the engine and machine, dust, vibration and the sun, and often worked long and uncomfortable hours if the corn was fit to be cut. Four tables were available with effective cutting widths from 3.35-5.17m (10"-16").

CENTRE RIGHT: This 2wd MF 135 tractor is towing a MF34 seed drill. This places corn at a predetermined rate in shallow grooves created by the machine, and then covers it. Fertiliser is also metered and placed alongside the seed at the same time.

BELOW RIGHT: This 105 hp (78kW) tractor was popular when it was in production in the mid 1970s . It used a 'multipower' transmission system, and gave 12 forward and four reverse gears. This tractor is not fitted with either a rollbar or a safety frame on the cab. One or other of these is now obligatory for driver safety.

TOP and ABOVE: New Holland's Series M was introduced in 1996. The M160 tractor is powering a Maschio tiller at the front, which is driven directly from the front of the engine for max efficiency. A second Maschio cultivator is to the rear. This range of four tractors (the M160 being the largest) are fitted with naturally aspirated or turbo-charged engines developing 100hp (74kW) to 160hp (119kW). A wide range of transmissions are available, to give forward speeds from 0.23kph. to 40kph.

RIGHT: The series M tractor cab. This illustration shows how the narrow, tapered bonnet, thin cab pillars and a tapered instrument console maximise driver visibility. The main driver controls are on the right.

ABOVE: The gear-change control for the New Holland series M. The two buttons on the top of this arm control up and down powershifts. A third, on the front of the lever, allows gear ranges to be changed. Signals from this lever operate electronically controlled and modulated hydraulic clutch packs, enabling the driver to change gear without using the clutch pedal.

ABOVE: The NH 6635, from the series 35, is one of a range of five tractors launched in 1996, ranging from 65-95hp (44-70kW). The 6635 is rated at 85hp (63kW). A low- to medium-power tractor, it is suitable for general farm work. A wide range of transmissions are available for different applications, including a 'creeper' option to give a speed as low as 300 metres per hour. These slow speeds are essential for some types of work, e.g. the operation of planting machines in a market garden.

RIGHT: The model 570 NH small rectangular baler is illustrated here. These machines still have a place on some farms, especially where the manual handling of bales is desirable. They will bale hay or straw and will produce a bale with a cross section of 36x46cms; length is adjustable.

ABOVE: A NH D1210 big square baler. These bales are preferred by large farms and contractors because of their handling and stacking advantage (illustrated by the lorry and trailer in the background). This machine produces a bale of 120x90cm and up to 2m long. The bales can weigh between 420kg (straw) to 750kg (silage).

LEFT: The NH Roll-Belt Baler, models 644 and 654. These machines produce the now familiar large, round bales, 1.2m wide, and either up to 1.5m or 1.8m in diameter. These machines are much cheaper to buy than the large square baler. The bales are mechanically handled and, despite appearances, stack reasonably well. These tractors will bale straw, hay or silage.

TOP: One of the last combines produced by Ransome's, the Cavalier was fitted with a Ford six-cylinder diesel engine and a 12" or 14" table. It weighed about 5.4 tonnes and was, slightly unusually, fitted with a primary threshing drum, which claimed to do about 20% of the threshing.

ABOVE: Another view of the Ransome's Cavalier combine. The operator talks to the farmer before the day's work, mid- to late-morning when the moisture content in the grain is at its lowest.

LEFT: It is important that modern tractors can handle many different attachments. This means that the rear hitches have to be easily accessible, easy to use and durable. A variety of hitches are available for each market, as shown on this Renault tractor.

BELOW: Renault is the leading French tractor manufacturer and has consistently shown itself to be open to new developments, and it was one of the first companies to introduce fuel-economy displays in the driver's cab. Today it continues to produce both specialist and general-purpose tractors, including a range especially designed for orchards and vineyards.

ABOVE: This 85hp Renault Ceres tractor is pulling a four-harrow reversible plough. It can be fitted with four different synchromesh gearboxes, depending on requirements, the basic model giving 10 forward and 10 reverse speeds.

RIGHT: A view of the working position in the driver's cab of the Renault Ceres range of tractors. There is good, unobstructed access to the door for entry and exit. In common with most agricultural tractors, two brake pedals are fitted for independent operation of the left- and right-hand brakes, to reduce the turning circle. These are locked together for road use.

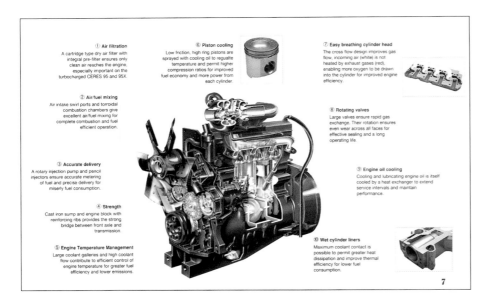

The various callout labels in the engine diagram read:

① Air filtration
A cartridge type dry air filter with integral pre-filter ensures only clean air reaches the engine, especially important on the turbocharged CERES 95 and 95X.

② Air/fuel mixing
Air intake swirl ports and torroidal combustion chambers give excellent air/fuel mixing for complete combustion and fuel efficient operation.

③ Accurate delivery
A rotary injection pump and pencil injectors ensure accurate metering of fuel and precise delivery for miserly fuel consumption.

④ Strength
Cast iron sump and engine block with reinforcing ribs provides the strong bridge between front axle and transmission.

⑤ Engine Temperature Management
Large coolant galleries and high coolant flow contribute to efficient control of engine temperature for greater fuel efficiency and lower emissions.

⑥ Piston cooling
Low friction, high ring pistons are sprayed with cooling oil to regualte temperature and permit higher compression ratios for improved fuel economy and more power from each cylinder.

⑦ Easy breathing cylinder head
The cross flow design improves gas flow, incoming air (white) is not heated by exhaust gases (red), enabling more oxygen to be drawn into the cylinder for improved engine efficiency.

⑧ Rotating valves
Large valves ensure rapid gas exchange. Their rotation ensures even wear across all faces for effective sealing and a long operating life.

⑨ Engine oil cooling
Cooling and lubricating engine oil is itself cooled by a heat exchanger to extend service intervals and maintain performance.

⑩ Wet cylinder liners
Maximum coolant contact is possible to permit greater heat dissipation and improve thermal efficiency for lower fuel consumption.

7

TOP LEFT: The Renault Ceres tractor engine shown is a four-cylinder direct-injection diesel, fitted with a turbocharger mounted on top of the engine. This is an exhaust-gas-driven turbine, which drives a fan which blows more air into the engine to raise power output.

CENTRE LEFT: A disadvantage with large front-wheeled 4wd machines can be an increased turning circle due to the restricted movement available for the larger wheels. The option illustrated is a good compromise, using large wheels but still achieving a good steering lock.

BELOW LEFT: This machine is fitted with a front-end loader, operated by the tractor's hydraulics, which in turn may have a wide variety of attachments. This one is designed for handling round bales.

ABOVE: Vineyard tractors have been made by most manufacturers, and are very narrow versions of the basic machine, designed for going between rows of vines. This Renault model is shown applying chemical dust for pest control.

RIGHT: This tractor is one of 11 fruit and vineyard models manufactured by Renault. The smallest in the range is just under 1m in width. Because of this reduced track width, they are unsuitable for traversing slopes, as they are unstable.

RIGHT: The Renault fruit and vineyard tractors are fitted with three- or four-cylinder direct-injection air-cooled diesel engines.

BELOW: For some operations like harvesting, fruit and vineyard tractors have to travel very slowly. They can therefore be supplied with a transmission system to give a minimum forward speed of 450 metres per hour.

ABOVE: This Renault tractor, fitted with dual wheels at the rear to reduce soil compaction, is preparing a seedbed and planting seed for next year's crop. Its transmission has three speed ranges (creep, field and transport), which are initially selected by the driver. A further nine gears are available within each of these ranges, which can be hydraulically changed by the driver while on the move.

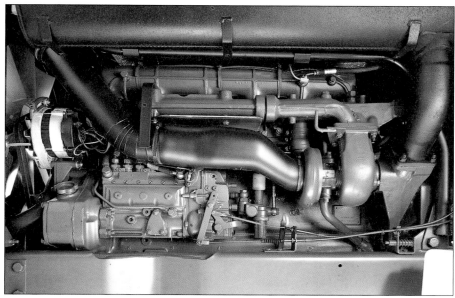

ABOVE: One of the engines used in the Renault Multishift range of tractors, fitted with a turbocharger and an in-line fuel-injection pump. This injects diesel at high pressure — about 180 kg/cm^2.

TOP: This 4wd Renault tractor is fitted with dual wheels to reduce soil compaction. It is towing a large set of disc harrows to start preparing a seedbed.

ABOVE: Ceres 95X Spacial (85hp, 63 kW) planting wheat, fitted with a power harrow/seed-drill combination unit

RIGHT: An 80-14 fruit tractor (76 hp) bringing fruit in from the orchard.

LEFT: A Ceres 95X Spacial, with fitted front loader and silage.

TOP: A 180-94TZ (170hp 125kW) shown baling straw with its CLAAS baler attachment.

ABOVE: A Renault 106-54TL (100hp, 75kW) and disc harrows cultivating stubble ground.

ABOVE: Popular in the late 1970s and 1980s, RECO's self-loading forage trailer was designed as a one-man silage-making operation. It would pick up a cut crop, chop it and load it into the trailer. The cutting action was achieved by forcing grass past 21 stationary knives, giving a 65mm chop length, which aided compaction in the silage clamp. The crop was unloaded by slats in the floor moving it
rearwards when the tailgate was opened at the silage clamp.

RIGHT: The front-mounted and trailed versions of RECO's Fella Turbo Disc-Mower are illustrated here, each of which have a 3m cutting width and can cover 3.5ha per hour. Each machine has six discs fitted with two knives per disc; these rotate at high speed, cutting the grass, and putting it into a swath.

The 'Storti' Bulldog mixer wagon is designed to weigh animal feed accurately as it is loaded into the hopper, and to mix all the ingredients thoroughly together. The feed is ejected through a discharge gate and is then elevated to a feed trough. This is filled evenly as the tractor draws the mixer wagon along its length.

ABOVE: Large, round bales of hay, straw or silage, ideal for on-farm handling, are produced by the Gallignani baler. When used for silage, the bales need to be totally sealed in plastic by the Autowrappa 3; this prevents the deterioration of the fodder and maximises the feed value.

ABOVE: Made by Ruston's Engineering Co (RECO) of Huntingdon, this Feeda trailer is used for putting animal feed into troughs. It has a chain-and-slat type moving floor, which slowly moves the feed to the front of the trailer. Here it passes through steel beaters, which shred out the material and feed it onto a conveyor belt which discharges the feed into the trough as the tractor moves forward.

PREVIOUS PAGE: These fly-wheel type precision-chop forage harvesters, produced for RECO by Mengele, are used to cut forage into short lengths, altered according to requirements from 4 to 17mm. The shorter the chopped length, the better the compaction in the silage clamp, thus providing better quality silage. With maize, short lengths are essential: animal digestive systems cannot cope with whole seeds. This machine is available trailed (illustrated) or front-mounted, and can be fitted with special attachments for maize, or to pick up grass.

ABOVE: These machines are designed to spread fertiliser accurately and evenly over their working width. Hopper capacities from $0.27m^3$ to $3m^3$ are available. The DPX 1504 Sulky fertiliser spreader illustrated has a capacity of $1.5m^3$

TOP RIGHT: This six-cylinder 74kW (102hp) SAME 100.6 tractor is fitted with the company's 'Agroshift' gearbox. Like most modern tractor gearboxes, this will give the wide range of forward speeds that are essential for optimum efficiency. This gearbox has four ranges.

BELOW RIGHT: A SAME Silver 90 exudes much the same sort of appeal as an exotic sports car outside an Italian bar. Noted for its lifting capacity of 4,700kg, the Silver has a top speed of 40kmh on the road.

ABOVE: SAME, based in Treviglio, Italy, was founded in 1942 by Francesco Cassani, a designer who had started work in his father's workshop, and who later became a leading specialist in diesel engines. Building his first diesel tractor in 1927, Cassani produced a small range of water-cooled engines which were started by compressed air. Production ceased during the 1930s, but after the formation of SAME Trattori, the company went from strength to strength, later acquiring Hurlimann and Lamborghini. The Leopard 90 turbo, produced by SAME, was available with either 2- or 4wd. It was fitted with an 88hp (65kW) four- cylinder diesel engine. It

had a single-plate dry-friction double clutch, and 12 forward and three reverse gears. The PTO clutch was hydraulically operated, multi- plated and oil immersed. Hydraulic three point linkage had lower link depth-control sensing, not a common contemporary feature for a tractor of this size.

ABOVE: Handbuilt by Schlüter in Bavaria, these tractors were marketed in the UK by Ruston's Engineering Co (RECO) of Huntingdon during the early 1980s. They ranged in power from 115hp to 240hp (86-179kW).

RIGHT: The Schlüter tractor cab, as well as its bonnet, tilts to give good access to the machine for servicing and repairs, without disconnecting any of the controls or service systems.

The Väderstad combined cultivator/seed drill is shown folded ready for road transport. The caterpillar tractor pulling it is mounted on rubber tracks which reduce ground pressure and therefore soil compaction, and can therefore safely be driven on public roads without damaging the surface.

TOP and BOTTOM LEFT: This Väderstad cultivator and seed drill also has separate fertiliser and seed hoppers, but the metered quantities of seed and fertiliser are blown to the coulters that form a groove into which the seed is placed. The machine can be folded for road transport to a width of 3m.

ABOVE: This seed and fertiliser cultivated drill, produced by the Swedish firm, Väderstad, has following wheels which press the soil around the seed after it has been planted. This promotes even germination. The tractor pulling the drill is fitted with very wide tyres to reduce the overall soil compaction.

LEFT: A cultivator/drill from the Väderstad Rapid 300 and 400 range. The operator is showing the hoppers in which the fertiliser and seed are held, and from which it is is metered and gravity-fed for planting. The dividable wall is also adjustable, to accommodate different ratios of seed and fertiliser. The plastic cover keeps them dry, as wet fertiliser can clog the machine.

ABOVE: The Väderstad Rapid RD 300P.

PHOTO SOURCES

Bamfords 7
Bustatis 7
David Brown/Case 8, 9
CLAAS 10, 11, 12, 13, 14, 15, 16, 17
Deutz-Fahr 1, 18, 19, 20, 21, 22, 23, 24, 25
Fiat 26
Fendt 27
Ford 28, 29, 30, 31
International 32
JCB 33, 34, 35, 36, 37, 38
John Deere 39, 40, 41, 42, 43, 44, 45, 46, 47, 48, 49 (Top)
Kuhn 49 (Bottom), 50, 51

Lamborghini 52
Leyland 53
Morooka 54, 55
Maschio 56
Massey Ferguson 2, 57, 58, 59, 60, 61, 62, 63, 64, 65, 66
New Holland 67, 68, 69, 70, 71
Ransomes 71
Renault 72, 73, 74, 75, 76, 77, 78, 79, 80, 81
RECO 82, 83, 84, 85, 86
SAME 87, 88
Schlüter 89
Väderstad 90/91, 92, 93, 94, 95

LEFT: How things have changed! International harvester TD-8 with caterpillar tracks.